A  in the Water – *Candice James*

I flew wingless
inside a vacuum of nerves ...

I'm still tingling —

tingling.

(excerpt pg. 16)
Sensations in Bright

Also, by Candice James

Print Books
Transitioning
10 PAK – 5;10 PAK-4; 10 PAK-3; 10 PAK-2; 10 PAK-1
A Potpourri of Paintings;
The Still Small Voice of Soul;
Spiritual Whispers; Atmospheres;
Blue Silence; Call of the Crow;
Imagination's Reverie; Short Shots 2;
The Depth of the Dance;
Behind the One-Way Mirror;
The Path of Loneliness
Rithimus Aeternam; The Water Poems;
Short Shots; City of Dreams;
Merging Dimensions; The 13th Cusp;
Colors of India; Purple Haze;
A Silence of Echoes; Shorelines; Ekphrasticism;
Midnight Embers; Bridges and Clouds;
Inner Heart, a Journey; A Split in the Water

10 FREE e-books www.ebooks.net/poetry/Abstrusion
Abstrusion; Wonderland; Fract & Flect;
Year of Divine Madness; 60 Haiku;
Midnight Shootout; Naked Leavings
The Rising; CJ Poetry & Paintings;

https://www.everand.com/author/572119332/Candice-James

A ~~SPLIT~~ in the
WATER

Candice James

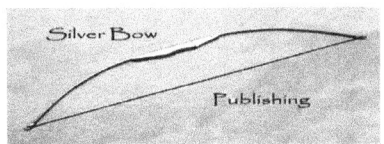

Silver Bow Publishing
720 Sixth Street, Unit # 5
New Westminster, BC
CANADA V3L 3C5

Title: A Split In The Water
Author: Candice James
Copyright © 2025 Silver Bow Publishing
Cover Painting: "Moonlight Bay" painting by Candice James
Layout/Design: Candice James
ISBN: 9781774033951 (print)
ISBN: 9781774033968 (ebk)j

All rights reserved including the right to reproduce or translate this book or any portions thereof, in any form except for the use of short passages for review purposes, no part of this book may be reproduced, in part or in whole, or transmitted in any form or by any means, electronically or mechanically, including photocopying, recording, or any information or storage retrieval system without prior permission in writing from the publisher or a license from the Canadian Copyright Collective Agency (Access Copyright)

© Silver Bow Publishing 2025
ISBN: 9781774033951 (print)
ISBN: 978177403396-8 (ebk)j

Library and Archives Canada Cataloguing in Publication Title: A split in the water / Candice James. Other titles: Split in the water (Compilation) Names: James, Candice, 1948- author. Description: 2nd edition. | Previously published: Fredericton, N.B.: Fiddlehead Poetry Books, 1979. | The word "split" appears with a strike through it on source of information. Identifiers: Canadiana (print) 20250319861 | Canadiana (ebook) 20250321017 | ISBN 9781774033951 (softcover) | ISBN 9781774033968 (Kindle) Subjects: LCGFT: Poetry. Classification: LCC PS8569.A429 S65 2025 | DDC C811/.54—dc23

Author's Note

A Split in the Water was my first book of poetry, published in 1979 by Fiddlehead Poetry Books, University of New Brunswick. It went out of print some time ago. Throughout, the copyright remained with the author.

I was reading through the book a few days ago and decided to revive it and have it available for sale in the worldwide market place through Silver Bow Publishing and Ingram Worldwide Distribution.

It is 99 ½ percent the same as the original... the only changes, are some punctuation and line breaks and a few, very few poems culled.

Fred Cogswell was the editor of Fiddlehead Poetry Books and a founding member of the League of Canadian Poets. I am forever grateful to him for believing in my poetry. Had he not published this book I may never have continued down the path of poetry and would never have become Poet Laureate Emerita of New Westminster, BC CANADA. Thank you, Fred!   ~ *Candice James*

**Dedicated to
the memory of Fred Cogswell**
Fiddlehead Poetry Books

(November 8, 1917 – June 20, 2004)

**Thank you for publishing
my first book of poetry in 1979**

Contents

Whose Footprints / 11
He Knows / 12
A Double-Bladed Brush / 13
Waves Washing / 14
Mind Diagrams / 15
Sensations in Bright / 16
Casual Thoughts / 17
Magic Mirror / 18
Strange Familiar Residence / 19
Mirror Exchange / 20
Walking / 21
System / 22
Small Portions / 23
Broken-Winged Lament / 24
All Dressed Up With Nowhere to Go / 25
Mistrial / 26
Test Drive / 27
Belated Spring / 28
Sleeping Searchlight / 29
Centrefold / 30
Night Network / 31
The Long Walk / 32
Looking Back / 33
Decibel Rhythm / 34
Disco Fever / 35
Raw Red Nightmare / 36
Screaming Streamers / 37
A Split in the Water / 38
Jet Lag / 39
The Promised Land / 40
Lifeline / 41
A Slight Miracle / 42
The Unreleased / 43
Snow Violets / 44
Unarrested / 45
Golden Green Eyes / 46
A Fool's Fool / 47
Bleeders / 48
Focal Point /49

Sun Touching / 50
Surrenders / 51
The Devouring / 52
Fragrances / 53
The Consummation / 54
Colder / 555
Trick Gambler / 56
Hairline Fracture / 57
Colours of Confession / 58
Going Broke / 59
Act Four - Scene Final / 60
Rosebuds and Snowflakes / 61
Advance Loan / 62
Final Phase / 63
Halfway Exits / 64
Casualty / 65
Splitting Apart / 66
Fading Winds / 67
Born Believers / 68
Killer / 69
When It Came / 70
And the Wound Cries Out / 71
Human Nightgown / 72
Fire-Gazing / 73
The End of a Living Poem / 74
Undefined / 75
A Venusian Embrace / 76
Escapade Ended / 77
In Need of a Filter / 78
If You Had Been a Welder / 79
Tombstone Territory / 80
The Operation's a Success / 81
Wall-Eyed Wheels / 83
Looking for a Reason / 84
Cameo Consort / 85
Supernatural Story / 86
Leftovers / 87
Split-Second View / 88
Cold Hands, Cold Heart / 89
Redemption in Red / 90
Each Night / 91

Lost / 92
Sacrifices / 93
Flowers / 94
Dream Drifting / 95
Blue Days/ 96
Actions / 97
Bible Story / 98
Graven Images / 99
Entrances / 100
The Absence of Sound Wave / 101
A Song is a Song / 102
Temporary Jailbird / 103
Windows, Cupboards and Bizarre Brown Chairs / 104
Silent Dream / 105
Ninety-Six Eyes / 106
Tarantula Trek / 107
Replacements / 108
A City Sleeping / 109
Iceberg Horses / 110
Artificial Eyes / 111
Alive for a Day / 112
Music Spheres / 113
Many Dreams Ago / 114
Suspension Bridge / 115
Bathroom Blues / 116
Sewn / 117
The Winds of Change / 118
Blotters / 119
Showers and Dust / 120
These Wolves /121

Author Profile / 122

A ~~Split~~ in the Water – *Candice James*

Whose Footprints?

Our footprints run parallel
in a criss-cross pattern of need.
Cinnamon-stick characters
strolling through bakeries
imprisoned in apple pie scenes.

Structures of flour harden to ice cubes
in ovens that self-destruct.
We're baked in a cheese loaf
and clicked through a camera
then sliced into bits.

> We're construed in a sandwich
> then chewed through a thought
> of indiscreet indigestion.

> The question —
> Whose footprints are whose?

He Knows

He knows.
                He never says a word but
he knows.
                It amazes me how
he knows
                when not even
I know
                for sure.

He knows

I know
He knows.
                If he says NO,
                I'll make certain
He knows
                For sure.

A Double-Bladed Brush

Dancing through corduroy mountains
hillsides run from the sea

Clouds gather grey
like industrial smokestacks at bay.

Death chokes life in her wake.

Seasons file through
on broken bicycle wheels,
       Circular robberies
          of some confused calendar.

Feelings cut through the painting
like a double-bladed brush

Waves Washing

Waves wash on the crux of human emotion:

       Waves rolling.
       Waves ebbing.
       Waves breaking.

The tides of human love
are ever changing.

       A raging sea can start love
       and end it.

       Waves wash some hearts
       and drown others.

Mind Diagrams

I calculate numbers
in terms of exponent eels.
I compute my frivolity
against the fears running rambunctiously
over my headgear.

Mouths frown at my carefully clothed body.

Feet writing with pens
to complete Christmas card orders pity me.

I am captured in my tomb of freedom
giving up my wrists and ankles
to angels of malice.

Burning ashes inside an iceberg,
I view the world from inside-out.
A pineapple upside-down cake,
confused and twisted,
encased in a frozen terrarium.

Cautiously, I change into a flexible scream —

An angry eagle flying
the raging December seas,
I reverse slowly through childhood lakes.

For a fleeting instant, the storm subsides.

I see my reflection clearly,
buried in a bottomless pit
    of freedom.

Sensations In Bright

I picked a prancing tulip
and disturbed a peaceful star.
The tulip couldn't grow
without its roots of life.

The star that was a sentinel
disintegrated to space dust.
Skydiving like an ice skate
across a midnight sky.

A million voices whispered in awe
and bled through plastic veins.

I talked to a star
that answered no questions.
I danced with a tulip
that remained motionless.

I flew wingless
inside a vacuum of nerves...

        I'm still tingling —
            tingling.

Casual Thoughts

I think of pleasure casually.
Images of petals bursting
through a blue velvet carpet
of sensual caresses.

Scriptures of love letters
nestling in the ember-burning fireplace
of a memory.

> I think of love intelligently
> and act it out
> like some insipid play
> I'm starring in.

Perhaps if I were to think of love casually
I could come to better terms with its essence.

Magic Mirror

> *"Mirror, mirror on the wall*
> *Who's the biggest fool of all?"*

It doesn't answer.
Its magic has been murdered.

Even though I'm not a magician
I conjure up the heartbreaking answer.

> *"Mirror, mirror on the wall,*
> *I'm the biggest fool of all."*

Suddenly the mirror becomes momentarily magic

      and teardrops stain
      her refracted reflection.

Strange Familiar Residence

It's all so slow it's almost backwards
and then suddenly it reels forward.
You realize where you are.
You've been there for a thousand years
but everything is so unknown
that you shudder with fear.

Is it really the way it's always been?
Or only the way you dreamed it should be.

Unknown rescinded hallucinations
colour the landscape as far as the eye can see.
But now the mind can penetrate further
into the strange magical valleys
of known residence.

>You view it from inside out now
>and it seems so right in its transition.

And that is the way it always will be.

Mirror Exchange

You are not looking at me.
You're looking at my mirror image.
I was so weary of the world
I exchanged reflections
with slab of polished glass.

My new environment,
trapped in the shine of glass,
is more satisfying.

I change images
with every stranger
that stares through my maze.

I live intensely.
I reflect with passion.
I am the mirror.

An image —
that took flight
in the secret of night.

Walking

Walking casually, incoherently
and somehow, with that near miss,
we've managed to renovate ourselves
into a seemingly new discovery.

We are the third-grade inventors.
We are the second-hand inventions.
We are the first-degree frauds.

Walking past hope
our intersections have become
a jungle of tangled tomorrows.

Navigation, now,
is completely impossible.

System

In the land of miles
we inch forward
foot by foot.

        Armed with ice-cream idiosyncrasies
        We prove the jester's cause.

Bearing crosses on our chests
our souls heave with saving grace.

Never to be born new again,
we make do with our second-hand hearts.

        And we walk.
        And we run,

But we never reverse
through our forest of miniature miles.

        We are compounding inches
        in the land of decimal points.

Small Portions

The chicken was basted
with cherished hopes.

The potatoes were sautéed
in the pan of patience.

The broccoli was burned
in the bowl of bizarre coincidence.

The sunflower seeds were steamed
in the stove of sadness.

The turnips were
the temperature of tears.

Had my appetite been appropriate,
I would have picked up a feast of maturity
with a morsel of experience.

Broken-Winged Lament

I am trapped
      in an iceberg
when I should be in Capistrano.

      I'm a lost sparrow
          dying —
              dying.

If only
      I could find the room
         to flap my wings
      I could melt
      this layer of ice
         covering me,
         smothering me.

      But I'm trapped
      in an iceberg
when I should be in Capistrano.

All Dressed Up With Nowhere To Go

My jewellery box crashed to the floor
spilling necklaces, bracelets, and rings
        I'd forgotten I had.
My mood changed completely
      to a need for over-dressing.

I placed three rings on my left hand:
abalone, silver, and a cameo head.
Two watches and a bracelet around my left wrist:
A Timex, a Seiko, and a ten-carat chain of charms.

My right hand seemed naked without any stones.
I remedied that situation. A macramé ring,
a golden snake broach and three sparkling diamond gems.

Above these five rings I wore two charm bracelets.
Both were of sterling silver with baubles, bangles, and beads.

Still feeling a little undressed, I placed three golden pendants
        around my neglected neck.

Dressed in blue jeans and logger-type boots,
I walked out into the courtyard.
I leaned against my balcony to wait for pre-school to end.

A scruffy young boy gaped at me quizzically
"Hey lady, you're wearing two watches."

The manager and his wife ambled on by.
I heard him whisper to her
"That's the eccentric young writer; I told you about.
The one that lives with the old man
who can't talk English too good."

      All dressed up with nowhere to go,
      I watched my daughter running toward me.
        She thinks I'm beautiful.

Mistrial

The fever had broken
and recovery was instantaneously imminent.
Evidence was presented for prosecution.

The defence permanently rested in peace.
The jury was not sworn in.
The exhibits were unlabelled.

The courtroom was empty
The bailiff had no legs.
The recorder was without arms.

The witnesses were out to lunch
     at the closed restaurant.
         They hungrily ate the air
         and breathed the food.
They knew a life was hanging in the balance
so, they haplessly upset the scales.

The scales crashed to the floor
and smashed into a million pieces.

The puzzle created could never be fixed.

Recovery proved to be the stronger foe.
The fever agreed to unconditional surrender.

     The judge ruled a mistrial.
       And life went on
          and on ... and on.

Test Drive

You are a used Cadillac convertible.

      I found your keys,
      stepped inside,
      felt your plush interior.

I switched on your radio.
All stations, AM and FM, played only love songs.

I reached up and unsnapped your catches.
Your top sank down smoothly,
uncovering your secrets.
      I turned on your wipers
      and washed your tinted windows.
          I tried your headlights.
          They illuminated the dark.
          High beam was blinding.

I turned the ignition key and drove you a few blocks.
      The brakes were good.
      The gears were smooth.
      The steering was excellent.

      I looked at myself in the rear-view mirror
      and felt comfortable with the reflection.

          I decided to keep you
            even though you were used.

      They don't make cars the way they used to.
        Sometimes —
      the older models are better.

Belated Spring

The white flowing fur of winter
holds a strange warmth of its own.

It penetrates blackness
and its fingers of light unbutton the void,
unlacing the deepest hue of invisibility.

This thick fur,
covering a January earth with warmth,
has stolen my heat away.

              I'm naked,
              without fur,
              freezing in luxuriant flames,

              and flooding within
              my belated Spring.

Sleeping Searchlight

With hair of silk
and stars for eyes he walks into a dream.

He searches the whipped cream mountain tops
       for the cherry of his crops.

The whipped cream melts, menacingly,
to leave a cap of purple pits.

Just like a sundae without the ice-cream
       he cannot find his epitomized self.

He searches the foam filled landscape
for his residue of life.

The foam floats flagrantly away
to leave his thoughts undone.

       Just like a dog without a leash
       he cannot find his coveted castle.

He searches the limestone carpet quarry
for the element of gold.

The carpet cracks into a crumbling crevice
to leave an open centre.

       Just like a molecule without an atom
       he cannot find his singular self.

The searchlight searches for days and nights;
       then sleeps forevermore.

Centrefold

If I had to paint a picture
depicting the landscape of my heart
I'd have to use a schizophrenic scheme.

The left half of the painting would portray
a barren winter mountain-scape
dulled with blacks and greys.

The right side would be
a warm seashore scene
flowing with turquoise blue waters;

      And I would be,

    standing in the centre,

        unfolded.

Night Network

He is perched on the picket fence of extremes.
        His eyes glitter with moonlight.

        He eyes the grass
and it becomes a metamorphosis of dancing colours.
        He is captivated by the colours.

The nights swim by with obliquely,
        and still his eyes sparkle,
          lids opalescent and open.

His body is blemished and weary
        but still
his eyes twinkle more fiercely than stars.

Now the world starts swirling
in the undercurrent of his eyes.

        Victorious,
        vertigo plunges the land
        into a multi-coloured vortex.

His eyes are a whirlpool of wonder.
He is the disappearing marauder.

A gritty feeling in the eyes
is the only vestige left behind
by this subterranean sandman.

The Long Walk

The cold damp fog
invades the dew drenched fields
       then rolls
   onto my doorstep.

The cool grey mist enshrouds the view
and hides reality under her haze.

I walk inside her eyes...

It's like walking in an alien marshland
where signposts make no sense
and heavens can't be found.

Wet bushes are icy fingers
touching hair raised skin.

It's an almost blindness
that charts courses of confusion
surrounded by four grey walls.
          But
     stuck in the centre.

With leaden feet
I walk in constant chaotic circles
trying desperately to touch something
other than this dense drapery of fog.

Looking Back

Winter is here and I am homeless.

The summer passed too quickly.
Sunshine days are only a memory now.
My feet, a thawing silver, not grey.

    I'm standing nude in the sleet and rain
    in the middle of an abandoned ice field
      and yet I feel no chill.

Renegade dewdrops kiss my ankles into ice-cubes.

    I glide through the valley of mouths
      Un-swallowed.

    My eyes open to a vision.
    My arms open to a stranger.
    My heart opens to a feeling.

Looking back over my shoulder,
    I catch a glimpse of winter
      departing through glaciers.

  In front of me,
    the rising sun
is melting my ice field away.

Decibel Rhythm

I'll never forget the decibel reading!

We joined in perfect silence.
        A deafening amalgamation.

We were
elements of a separate merger
deliberately discharging each other
like a double-barrelled shotgun.

We were crafty:
Side-stepping the toughs.
        Vetoing the bluffs.

We were volatile:
        Gunpowder children
        dancing the discos of thunder,
        ripping the dancefloors asunder.

I'll never forget the look on your face
as I two-stepped away in the tango of time
and waltzed away from your uneven rhythm.

Even now
        I remember the decibel reading
        and the look on your face,

        But I can't remember
        the name of the song.

Disco Fever

Flashing, liquid lights.
Bouncing, beating music.
Masquerading rhythm.

Disco fever injects the atmosphere.
    Dancers come alive:
        Jumping, shuffling, bumping, grinding.

Cushioned floors stretch like elastic:
Hammered, stomped, battered, and bruised.

    Disco fever infects the dancers:
A disease running rampant, coughing contagiously.
    Virused ventilation, unvaccinated.

        The walls resound and reverberate.
        Pictures faint and fall.
        Walnut panels ripple and waver
            inside a disco dream.

    The clock ticks terminally.
        Time runs out.

    The music dies a quaffing death.
        Plexus severed.

Disco fever mounts to death;
    then drowns in time.

Raw Red Nightmare

Each dance step I take
Proves a clumsy experiment
      Falling over the moon
      Drowned on the shores of Tripoli.

I watch you, from my barstool,
parading your expertise
      inside a spotlight tango.

Applauding too hard I slip from my chair
and see myself fall from your grace.

Your face doesn't bless me.
Nor do your fingers
As I grasp for a thread from your heart.

Inside my raw red nightmare
I start a path of glory
that no one has seen before.

I release my vice grip
and see your weakened thread
reverberating in slow motion fade out.

My raw red nightmare is turning to gold
      as you slip stumble away
            inside a broken jazz waltz.

Screaming Streamers

The sunlight falls in streamers
         across
the vast green fields.

         Canary grass and bushes
         obscurely dot the warm green blanket
         like a uniform with egg-stains.

Animals graze in the pasture.
         Slow robots
                  with mechanical mouths.

         The sound of a dog barking
                  jumps through the grass
                           and gives life to the air.

The rustling trees
         s t r e t c h
                           their limbs
         and try to embrace the sky.

The mesmerized flowers
         crane their necks
         upward to the sun.

                  The farm comes alive.

A Split in the Water

Velvet red waters beckon me.
I dive into the glass of wine.
My blood is chilled
as it mingles with the warmth
of its essence.

Slowly I descend its liquid quality
and I become solid.

Darkness becomes more complete
       as the bottom of the glass
       comes into view.

I want to touch the bottom of oblivion.
I try desperately to plunge further downward
       as I am snatched from fantasy
       by strong hands and sure arms.

       They pull and prod at my soul.
       Firmly they capture my heart.

I am stunned and amazed
by the fierce electrification
of the swift journey upward and out.

The dark element has disappeared
and the automated light switch is engaged.

Sudden vision is blinding
                        then a blur
             and finally ...
        transparently clear.

Jet Lag

I feel your warmth.
I sense your exceeding heat.

>The roller coaster ride begins
>and speeds into overdrive.

Thrills and chills run rampant inside.

>Give me your split-second love,
>but only a particle or a fraction,
>>for a satisfied defeat.

I will love you for one quick moment in time.

>Please leave your hat on for Eternity.

>You'll be an object, a lover, and a friend
>as this feeling of feelings begins to end.

Exploration is followed by vagueness.
Vague feeling is supplemented by full emptiness.

>I know we were only meant to be
>for an instant or a second.

>>This I understood fully.

>It is my recognized acquaintance
>I accompany to total departure.

The Promised Land

The sweaters are empty now.
Closets are overflowing.

We were winter people.
       Violets growing in the snow.

Skateboard ceilings were our floors.
Blazing fireplaces were our doors.

       Sweating with every entry.
       Steaming with each departure.

Arrivals are always in airports underground.

Taking off our captain's hats,
we flew the tombs of time:
       Winged angels of death.
       Masked robbers of breath.

Caves yawned with boredom as we soared by.
       They captured us with closed mouths.

       Our wings fractured.

       With broken wings we flew
       into darkness
       and crashed on the sun.

       Burnt to a crisp
       in the promised land.

Lifeline

I look at it. I stare at it.
And I concentrate on it;
      but it cannot be seen.
      It has no shape.

I listen to it. I try to hear it.
And I await its music;
      but it cannot be heard.
      It is beyond the wavelengths
      of audible sound.

I try to touch it. I want to feel it.
And I grasp at it;
      but it cannot be captured.
      It is intangible.

I circumspect if from all sides.
Above and below. Within and without;
      but there is no beginning,
      no centre and no end.

            It is a form without a structure.
            It is an image without a thought.
            It is an unbroken thread
            unwinding from a never-ending spool.

            I try to define it
            and find it is far beyond human imagination
            and indescribably beautiful.

                  It is love.
               My love for you.

A Slight Miracle

Your eyes danced with a million possibilities;
                a ghost town of clouded colour.

I skated the ice-covered January sidewalks
                of your blue-green irises.

Moons rose over the daylight hills of passion.
           White, yellow, silver and gold.

You explored all of them
with your Geiger counter fingers.
           My frozen ice fields thawed
           under your radio-active emissions.

Your hair brushed my soul
and promised permanent tenure.

We appeared in the sky like a rainbow.
           Our colours blended;
              a spectacle of fireworks
                    in a hot midnight sky
                    after a lengthy monsoon.

A slight miracle was born in your eyes.
           It froze us into living statues
           burnt into this forever moment.

The Unreleased

The bed draws us in
        like heated circles.

        Your mouth is a satin ship
        covering my island.

We walk barefoot
exploring the plush carpet of our bodies,
            the fabric of our hearts,
            the texture of our souls.

        Our fingers swim with messages.
        They're beached on shores of braille.

We explode like colliding comets
        and blast through infinity
            successfully united.

        Impossible fusion.
        Burning fusion.
            Complete fusion.

We transfuse each other
        in a floating fortress
        of love personified.

        Impermanence is erased
        and we are fused together.

        We are the unreleased.

Snow Violets

I nearly woke up this morning
without remembering who I was
        or where I was going.

Then I saw the sparkling new key you gave me
        for all our tomorrows.

        Lovers unconsummated for so long
        soon to be united singularly.

        The sudden recall of all our buried kisses
        invokes disinterment immediate.
        The exhumation is ecstatic.

        Feverish future photographs
        flash through the button-hole scenery,
                key-holed into my door.

        I'll give you a fresh violet
                surrounded by snow.

                If you breathe on it...
                        it will live forever.

Unarrested

I remember you
perched on the ledge of the veranda:

>   Blue-green ocean background.
>   Gulls providing the detail.

You were sporting a black baseball cap
>   and a drunken grin.

>   Topless...
>   your curly gray-black chest hair
>   reached out
>   and grasped my fingers.

>   Hypnotic handcuffs closed over my wrists
>   crushing hot bones in ecstasy.

Now ... I'm trapped in the silk sheets
>   that cover your heart's bed.

>   Imprisoned forever
>   in a jungle of hair
>   searching for freedom's key.

>   The irony of it is:
I can't even remember being arrested.

Golden Green Eyes

His golden-green eyes of excitement
                are diamonds of the deep.

      Recesses of his stereo soul
              are reverberating whispers.

He's a coconut wineglass laced with pineapple;
        The finest exotic drink.

        I sup from his liquid,
        A fiery bath.
I burn in the warmth of his hands.

He's a palm tree beach in a luminous color.
            A roaring ocean shoreline scene.

            I trace his trails
            and climb his heights
            in a whirlpool of gentle waves.

He's a quick-change artist in silken sequins.
            A sequence of satin moods.

He's the impossible dream
soaked in sugar-sweet oil.
                Always slipping away.

I shift my gaze to his golden-green eyes.
Hypnotized by their red-hot flame
        my world is a cool blue ache.

A Fool's Fool

A fool
>needs only a little encouragement,
>>and you give it to me.

>You feed me with your fantastic lies
>>and bed me
>with your deceptive dreams.

How easily I thrive on your untruths.

>You tell me the moon is dark
>and somehow a cloud passes over it
>>and hides its light.

You tell me the sun doesn't shine
>and all i can see forever
>are dull gray skies.

You tell me water is not wet
>and i use it for a towel
>>to dry my tears.

>>You tell people don't breathe
>and I stand breathless
in suspended animation.

>You play me for a fool
>and I follow suit with eager ease.

>How easily you fool your fool
>>As only a fool can.

Bleeders

Bleeders —
    The world is filled with bleeders.
        Some bleed openly.
        Others in secrecy.

        Some require sympathy.
        Others indifference.

        Some bleed profusely.
        Others sparingly.

        Some require surgery.
        Others a band-aid.

The world is alive with knives
    that wound the bleeders:

        Steak knives.
        Carving knives.
        Stilettoes
          or
        Switchblades.

    The cut is still as fatal.

        Lust.
        Desire.
        Passion
          or
        Love.

    The cut is just as deep.

        Bleeders —
    The world is full of bleeders.

Focal Point

We held onto each other desperately.
      bound in Timex wristwatches:
          Shockproof. Waterproof.
We would always tick inside each other.

We spied a never-ending summer
through our well-crafted binoculars.

        Winter was non-existent:
      Under glass. Under ground.
          Through our eyes.

      We expelled all the seasons —
         save summer.

      We searched sandy beaches
    and warmed over waves for something
         still living and breathing.
           Nothing moved —
           No life.

We held onto each other and our perpetual summer
so desperately that we murdered all living creatures
      with a casual gaze from our blind eyes.

      We focused each other anonymously
        with laser beam optic nerves.

    We were alone in our macrocosm.

        And from our focal point ...
         it was enough.

Sun Touching

When I was a child
        I used to wonder
            what it would feel like
                to touch the sun.

I'm an adult now.

        I don't wonder
           anymore.

    I've touched your soul.

Surrenders

I want you to come to me unflagged
        in the deepest kind of surrender.

I want you to need me in every way
        with defeat serving ecstasy.

I will be Hitler and you be a Jew
        and we will end all atrocities.

I will love you like a raging fire
        but your soul will not be burned.

I will exalt you like a sovereign king
        and you will forgive me my sins.

I want you to come to me unflagged
        in the ultimate of surrenders.

The Devouring

He is so masculine and virile.
He puts Hercules and Achilles to shame.

I know with an ancient certainty
      that he is unreal.

He must be the ultimate illusion of flesh.

All men pale in his shadow
and become a mere shred of sexuality
      like an angle in a square
           not whole,
        only fragments.

He walks into the room
    after I've invented hours and years.
        and changes the months to minutes.

My eyes are all over him like fingers of fire
until he finally overshadows my view.

    I devour him inside my orifice of passion.
    No other human being may enter.

        We drown in our sea of love
        and savour the full devouring.

Fragrances

In this world
	there are so many fragrances

		But none so welcome
	as the sweet-smelling sweat
			from your body
		as it presses through mine.

The Consummation

When I lift my eyes up
        to gaze at a star-studded
                black midnight sky
      I am always amazed
             at the incoherent questions
             that pulse through my mind.

Questions that have no certain answers.

When I give my body over
        to your caresses
in the midst of a mounting fever
      I am always astounded
            at the gentle rage
                  that tenderly burns
           through my soul;
                a gentle fire
          that needs no fuel.

The birth of love
            is as perplexing
            as the birth of a universe.

      Both are conceived
            through creative need.

Colder

I found you
	breaking holes in the ice
		under a scorching summer sun.

You seemed so lonely.
I offered to chip the frozen snowflakes
	with you.

We laboured for days and nights
	shattering glass,
		gathering fragments,
			filling cube trays.

The seasons rumbled and echoed.
	We emptied our ice cubes
	onto the snowy sand,
		arranging and re-arranging them
		until the structure was perfect —
			finished.

Exhausted...
	we climbed into our seasoned igloo

		and still, we freeze,
		colder and colder.

			And I wonder ...
			who'll stop the cold?

Trick Gambler

It's like being at the crap-table in Vegas.
The odds are against your number coming up.

>But she's a gambler.
>She bets on the same number
>that screwed her time and time again.

It takes a lot of guts and a lot of stupidity.
>She's long on both.

>The chips are down.
>The bet is covered.
>The stakes are the highest.

>She throws the dice
>and time stops.

She sees the dice suspended.
The numbers are all there in clear view;
>— depending on your point of view.

>To win is impossible.
>To lose is improbable.

>The dice are loaded
>>on a 767.

>>With any luck at all
>>she'll break even.

Hairline Facture

You were really here all the time
               and now you're gone.
              Is it a short journey?
                A long trip?
     Or a complete rip in my universe,

Did I tug at the threads
        or did you pull at the seam?
              Can the torn threads be re-sewn
      or are the too weak for the fabric?

             Maybe it's not a rip.
Maybe it's just a hair lying in a straight line.

             Was it you or I
       that so casually shed that hair?
It must have been me because that one hair
is so dark against our white blanket background.

I can't find the tweezers. You must have them.

My fingers can't grasp the hair
but your tweezers can lift it off.
              The scissors of your heart
can also make the rip in my universe real.

Mend it with your needle
        or cut it with your scissors.
But don't make me hang
by a thread or a hair.

        Will you let me live in illusion
        or force me to cry in reality?

Colours of Confession

Red nail polish flecked on a satin white scroll.
Red semi-sweet sex on a sourdough roll.
Add sticky jam and some passionate love
and you can eat humble pie until you choke.
Surrender your heart for a barbeque roast.

Purple pillows on a cream velvet bedspread.
Purple love letters from a black sandstone heart.
Add phony phrases and some light lovely lies
and maybe you'll right a wrong melody.
Put your hope into gear on a runaway railcar.

Green galvanized waves on a bittersweet beach.
Green gabardine grass on a mist covered mountain.
Add wild winter wind and some northern chilled snow
and you can suffer the storm in a torn bathing suit.
Book your loose baggage on a perilous plane.

Young yellow flowers on a dark dirty doorstep.
Young yellow impulse on a taut tingling spine.
Add gloomy grey clouds and some nuclear nerves
and you can lose your second sight in a second.
Close your eyes on the roller coaster of rides.

Blue eyes searching through a majestic clear mirror.
Blue thoughts blossoming through a blanket of blame.
Add some emptiness and concrete confusion
and you can live your life lost on a desert island.
Take your soul to the limit of limitless life

Surrender your heart for a barbeque roast.
Book your loose baggage on a perilous plane.
Put your hope into gear on a runaway railcar.
Close your eyes on the roller coaster of rides.
Take your soul to the limit of limitless life
on the spaceship *"The Colours Of Confession"*
    and confess in the colours you are.

Going Broke

I've always been one

    For expensive hobbies:

        fancy cigarettes,
        single malt whiskey,
        luxurious limousines,
        private jets.
        genuine jewellery,
        haute couture

    and top of the mark restaurants

    to mention a few.

And now...

I've found a poverty-stricken partner

    who is partial to
    the same expensive tastes.

    We're both going broke
    in the wake of our love.

I guess that's what happiness
    is all about!

Act Four – Scene Final

Never in a few short months
        can you light up my life enough
        to illuminate all my future years.

The days cry out.
        "Release me. Release me."

All the lovers in history
        outshine us — even in dark hallways.

We tried in vain to light up the candles
        but the wicks were too short
        and our matches too wet.

I look around at our debris and wonder
        how I ever believed
     I could make a bed out of it
        or a life out of us.

With sheets and pillowcases in hand,
        I exit regretfully.

There's no one left
who cares enough to clap or applaud
our inept, lacklustre performance.

        Act Four – Scene Final.
          It's all over
        but the crying.

Rosebuds and Snowflakes

The immaculate brilliance
       of a rosebud blooming
         instantaneously
could give life
to conveniently blind eyes.

The thundering sound
of a gigantic snowflake
       crashing
could give hearing
to a seemingly deaf ear.

Why am I unable
       to get through
           to you?

Advance Loan

I drove expectantly to your house.
        The street was semi-blockaded:
        tractors, backhoes, jackhammers
            crashing and thrashing out
                their bizarre music.

Through an open window,
        I saw your face staring intently
        at the progressive industrial scene.

I wondered at your loneliness:
        Your dependence on me.
Your waiting to dream into my face.

        Love,
    without questions,
        accepting
a hundred unacceptable circumstances.

        I'll remove them soon.
I just bought some turpentine on credit.

I pay 72 tears a day…
            — without interest.

Final Phase

The banister of booze beckons him
to follow its merciless mate,
      the shallow staircase,
        to fate's final destination.

The birthday boy
lost track of meaningless,
mindless time.
much to his dismay.
He played a Jack
and lost a Queen
      In the game of *"Never Win."*

His wide, wet eyes
disguised the fool
who tempted fate too many times.

His eyes may dry at will,
but his future will flood forever
with famine.

His moods come and go
like busy buses
at the depot of despair.

A million chances minus six small zeros
      equate the number "one."
        AND...
    even a genius
    cannot transform "one"
    into miraculous "two"

Halfway Exits

We don't see eye-to eye.
        We don't fit cheek to cheek.
        We don't melt lips to lips.
        We don't beat heart to heart.

We live
an adequately pleasant existence
most of the time.

What we don't agree on,
we bury under a concrete carpet.

We've been burying so many differences
under that carpet lately
the floor should be ready to fall through soon.
        When it does, we'll say goodbye.

        It's really a shame
I've never really said hello to you
        since first we met.

        I guess I wasn't ready
        for an introduction.

        I was still only halfway
           through an exit.

Casualty

I eliminated you from my affections casually, coldly.
You rose from me like deflated smoke
unable to form rings in my atmosphere.

I severed the strings that tied us together
        in structured feelings of gauze.

You held a well-worn deck of cards in your hand.
        I wasn't interested in learning to play
            any more of your games.

Your broken puzzles never did fit
even when I tried to grin them together again.
Our wild, windblown nights turned motionless
with unoffered gifts, lost sentiments, buried emotions.

        A one-sided burial.
        I was your victim.
        You were my casualty.

I left you casually, coldly.

My departure resembled something...
        but it wasn't triumph.

Splitting Apart

The parting was beautiful.
        It could have been ugly, degrading,
                but it was beautiful:
Peace talks in the midst of battlefields.
Sun-drops in the centre of a snowstorm.

Her tears of guilt
over-brimmed her Stetson eyelids.
        He gently wiped them away.
With sympathetic looks
              he tried to ease the guilt
              imprinting itself
              on her pendulum heart.

        No harsh words.
        No cutting remarks.
              Only a simple kiss
              filled with understanding.

She turned from him
stepped into her vehicle and drove away.

Her rear-view mirror
still frames the indelible painting
of that day etched in her mind:

              He is standing at the barn door,
                A pipe in his mouth,
              his hands in his pockets,
                looking lost.

The splitting apart was beautiful...
    as beautiful as it could be.

Fading Winds

We were tied with uncertain strings
of dubious quality.

You tried so un-hard
that you fell on your shadow
and turned into black midnight dust.

Now...
I mind-search the wind
for a trace or a particle
of the you that you murdered so well —

The you
that has killed me so softly.

Born Believers

We should have signed a covenant
for we thought each other a God.

      If we had been born atheists,
      we might have made more sense of it.

            Born believers seldom endure.

Killer

If I were a fashion designer,
I'd draft you a beautiful casket;

    but I'm not.

I'm a funeral director
so, I'll perform a touching service
to commemorate your untimely death.

    I'm killing you tough
    with tender smiles,
      gentle words,
        and
    silent, satisfied laughter.

When It Came

When it came to games,
                a sure winner,
        you could always play for your dinner.

                When it came to love,
                like a heat wave,
        you pretended to burn in my flame.

When it came to the truth,
you tossed it around like a worthless toy
and giggled like a spoiled sneering boy.

                When it came to the point,
                a stiletto sharp knife,
        you cut your way out of my life.

And the Wound Cries Out

Orange orchids in the sun
    melt masqueradingly
    into two-faced tulips.

The diamond lying on my doorstep
    is only coal refined;
    coal as black as night
hiding a white lightning secret.

I love the lustre of the gem
while I question
its uncertain and dubious quality.

        The bottom of the top is clear
        as I circumspect its scope.

Yellow arms with green felt wrists
construct a rainbow railing outside the house.
    Blue lights and seashells glimmer.
Crabs cringe beneath translucent waves
    ss speedboats' roars and spume
    invade their gentle dreams.

    I cringe inside a lost love lament
as your misty memory pierces my helpless heart;
    and the wound cries out
    night after night after night.

And though the nights seem endless,
eventually... daylight must break through.

    Life rotates in the balance
    like a teak tree in the ocean.

Human Nightgown

I had a frosty dream last night:

I was looking
       for my warm cozy nightgown
              but I couldn't find it.

I searched the universe
       for my original sleeping habit
but somehow it continued to elude me.

       Then I woke up
and my nightgown was actually gone.

Where have you hidden my warmth?
       And why did you leave me?

I'm freezing through midnight
       without you.

Fire-Gazing

I am sitting
      before the blazing fire
           toasting my soul
           and eating poetry.

Your image blazes
           in my mind.
      as your eyes roast my heart.

Poetry becomes ineffectual.

    Fire-gazing
        and love blazing,
   toasting ...
        and roasting
           the soul.

The End of a Living Poem

I watched your heart shattering
      under my vocal fire.

      Each piece pulsated
         still glowing
    with the effort to sustain life.

      I watered your fire
with my perforating poetic oratory.

    And now,

        the poem is ending
     in unison with our fading fire.

Undefined

Lips
>were meant to be kissed.

Breasts
>were meant to be fondled.

Genitals
>were meant to be caressed.

Hearts
>were meant to feel love.

>Without you

>I have lost my meaning.

>I am
>>undefined.

A Venusian Embrace

A Venusian embrace
might have been what you needed.

I tried to hold you
       in the embrace of my arms,
          but I only smothered you.

            If I had the features
          of Venus Di Milo,
      I might have been able to hold you.

Escapade Ended

I am running away from you so hard
that every window on every street
shines with the image of your face.

>All my avenues of escape
>converge on the street you are.

I am trapped in my escape.

>The escapade ends
>— before it begins.

In Need of a Filter

If my heart had come equipped
with an activated charcoal filter,
        I could have kept dirt like you out.

After you infiltrated
ninety-nine percent
of my life force,
        I was close to cyanide poisoning.

                BUT...
      one percent was enough.

It became a Samson over the rest
and brought down
the temple of corruption
I was mired in.

The tumultuous crash
was my future foundation.

        This time,
I'll buy an activated charcoal filter
   to attach to my pacemaker.

             God...
      lead me not
   unto microwave ranges.

If You Had Been a Welder

The distance
             was too far
       for your rivet to hold me.

Had you been a welder
we might not have
         come   apart
            at the seams.

Tombstone Territory

It is a tombstone
in a territory without borders,
in a castle without ancestors.
The fireplace is embers
heating the dust-riddled furniture.

    Perversity fills the room
    with a strange enchantment.
It is reflected in the mirror of the century.

    Boredom overcomes
as you see yourself in perpetual reflections.
You dive into the refraction of the light
    and swim inside the mirror's pool.

        You are transparent.
        The mirror is your closet.

    Is it as deep as a tomb
    Or is it as shallow as life?

You are enveloped.
The prism closes over your being.

    Now you are the mirror.
You become an image, an unreality.

You try desperately to indicate love
    in a tremulous fit of apoplexy.
The tombstone crumbles,
    forms a mirrored wheel
    and rolls toward new territory.

        Tombstone territory.

The Operation's a Success

I

You're the pathologist in black
performing the delicate heart surgery.

I am the operating nurse
assisting on the removal
of your malignant brain tumor.

We are so adept with our unskilled fingers
       and our drugged-up minds.

Your surgical gloves are black
and I am dressed in stripes of grey matter
and crimson blood vessels.
Your bruised ego filters through your eyes
and the patient dies of respiratory love malfunction.

      Suddenly we become an emergency team.
      You pound the chest with your glass fingers.
      I give mouth to mouth resuscitation
      with my carbon dioxide lung offerings.

      The scalpel is screaming
"Recovery. Recovery. You are my victim."

      Love expired on the delivery room table.
      It was excreted
      through the intestines of our pupils.

      The cataracts laughed hysterically
      as the lids were stuck shut
      in the glue-like gauze
       of our overgrown wasteland.

      Crap unto crap...
is not spoken of human pride.

II

Early in the evening we, the executioners,
donned our clansman's hoods
and attended the funeral of our own creation...
                or cremation.

      It was a clear concise night,
      preceded by a gloom ridden day.

            The coffin had a traffic light
            for left turn only.

You skidded on the cloverleaf
and crashed into oblivion
when you insisted on going straight
against the left turn signal.

III

Another burial to attend.
      Shall I wear grey or black...
          or blood red?
      Only my pathologist can tell me
the wrong answer.

I nurse my pathologist
      with a scalpel for a pacifier
in the coffin of my cerebral cemetery.

      The operation's a success!

      Life unto death...
      is spoken of love.

Wall-Eyed Wheels

Summer lightning
strikes the solstice.
The seasons break apart.
Winter sunshine
warms the cold rain
that drowns the restless heart.

Corduroy blue jeans wrap the legs
that walk inside the snow.
Rose-coloured glasses frame the eyes
that search the candleglow.

The nicest flower lives in the pot
inside your own back fence.

The lamp that lights the dead of night
    illuminates your residence.

Looking for a Reason

Why
        am I allowed to lie soothingly
            in this warm relaxing bath
    when other people
            are freezing in the rain?

Why
        am I safe and comfortable
            inside my portable womb
    when other people
            are hurting without peace?

Sometimes...
        it rains
            all over the world.

Sometimes...
        it's dry
            in spots;

        but
        the rain in my heart
        started last night

            and it's flooding
            all of my streets.

Cameo Consort

I am travelling
Inside a multi-coloured pampas grass forest.
The scenery is both inspiring and stimulating.

    Is this what dreams are made of
                Miss Kingswood?

O talented advisor
and saviour of oddball entities,
search your skull for the mind-blowing answer
I can't compute.

How in Hades did a normal girl like you
ever become digested
in my insane, infrasonic, cerebral station?

How many eons ago
would I have withdrawn from breathing
if I had forgotten your timeless telephone number?

My criminal cadaver
       fills with concave compunctions.
They focus themselves
       like a jumbled alphabet soup scoresheet.

       After many frustrating
       and uncertain jig-saw hours,
          I phone you up,
    hoping that maybe together
we can crack this seemingly incalculable
       calculus code.

Supernatural Story

Merlin waved his magic wand,
      invoked incantations,
          and supernatural smoke swirled.

Cinderella and Prince Charming
vaulted from their prison's pages.
They were so weary of the same old lines,
      dreary dreams,
         and well-known scenes.

No hand holding now.
No lip lingering kisses.
      No familiar embraces,
    or casual caresses.
          No more happy ending.

                Only a beginning.
                  A splitting apart.
              A searching need.
          A burning desire
    to separate soft story book dreams
from reality's non-fiction hardcovers.

Merlin madly conjured
        and cast another spell.

    He materialized…
   a sequel.

Leftovers

Warm yellow sunlight streaking diagonally
across rustic brown sheets.

Warm water splashing vivaciously
into a beckoning bathtub.

Fluffy pink towels whispering
and wrapping themselves around
a fast-drying body.

Come hither coffee pot noises
nestling in the cozy corners of a thirsty thought.

Maple cupboard doors creaking open,
displaying invitational mosaic, mocha mugs.

Multi-coloured paper
cautiously covering party favor cigarettes
that call caressingly.

A plush brown velvet easy chair
merrily prances into the room
and winks you into its cuddly cushions.

It's another warm way
to face the morning's
chilled curriculum.

Split-Second View

The cloverleaf within the turn
                is on the outside now.

The circle turned inside itself
                and made a spiral view.

The sun shone down upon the view
                and made it come alive.

The trees ran hand in hand with plants
                as flowers danced around.

The buildings yawned with great relief
                and stretched their stifled studs.

The hedges and the shrubbery
                flexed full their leafy arms.

The logs and pebbles on the beach
                relaxed into the sand.

The clouds as silent sentinels
                smiled down upon the ground.

                The second split and passed in time.
        The circle spiralled back.
The pale sun disappeared from view

        And then ... the view was still.

Cold Hands, Cold Heart

Cold hands. cold heart.
Iceberg season is officially open.

Here come the hunters
with their thermal underwear
and hot water bottles.

Bated breath fogging up the landscape.
       Impaired vision sans alcohol.

Teeth break on frozen potato chips.
       Dips have turned to stone.

No refreshments tonight,
Or any other night
in iceberg territory.

Glacial eyes complement the landscape
and turn the hunters into statues
       beneath a midnight sun.

Cold hands, cold heart
       reign supreme.

Redemption in Red

Randy, red nail polish
    quite contrasting
    against a masculine body.

Gliding fingertips;
    silken threads
    caressing harvest hair.

Hungry wet lips
            touching,
            pressing:
    Heated irons on fabrics of the mind.

Hummingbird hands
    gently grasping,
    firmly forcing skin to melt.

Exquisite excitement slowly mounting
        pinnacles of passion
        to a pulsating peak.

    The lovers
        flow and float;
        then sink
            through the needle's eye.

    Wrapped in a cloud of tranquility —
        the redeeming residue
            of need's atrophy.

Each Night

Each night
        they exchange arms and legs.
        They star in each other's dreams.

        Each morning, they sip coffee
        through the same straw
        and gaze through each other's eyes.

Telephone wires have no meaning in their lives.
        Intricately and invisibly wired together,
        they share their united thoughts.

        They dress each other
        in threads of love and tenderness.

        They walk past mirrors
        and see no reflection.

Light essence is trapped inside them.
Rays refract and bend to suit their own needs.

Each night
        They exchange bodies and souls.
        Their love is energized.
        They are each other's battery.

        Life is co-existential.
        Everything else is unrequired —
                each night.

Lost

A daughter of the wild wind
she has no time for gentleness.

She soars blue skies and finds new suns.
Her thoughts and dreams
are coded through the stars.

She flows through summer nights,
a phantom breeze of endurance.
gusting with silver smiles and golden tears.

Waterfalls from distant planets
sing songs of love to her.
She applauds with thunder
then flows away in currents of air.

A gentle rustle,
        present through all eternity,
          she never completely arrives
            or departs.

She is lost love
searching for a familiar face
    buried deep
in the tomb of her memory.

        She is:
            Lost.

Sacrifices

All elements dissolve
and gather at her feet.
      She walks, hindered,
        through a two-foot high
        tangled jungle.

        Mad —
she's gone mad with the turns of humanity:

        Some riding.
        Some walking.
        Some sitting.
        But no-one sleeps.

      The need to find a mile
of clear transparent foot-space is too great.

She climbs through the trees,
  but there is no escape.
The jungle moss clings to her feet.

Moving like a turtle with no horizon in sight,
      she amputates her legs
      and fashions fleshy wings.

In the depth of her madness,
      playing with knives,
she carves a door for her escape
      and climbs out of herself...

      Flying, flying —
        finally, she's flying.

Flowers

Every day,
        fresh flowers stare at her
                from the oak tabletop.
      They talk to her
             but she doesn't hear
      the faint rustling of their leafy lips.

Every six minutes
they sing softly of forgotten melodies.
        An orchestration of pitiful petals.

She's not deaf,
but still, she hears not their musical quality.

She carefully paints her nails
with candy-apple red polish.

The flowers rustle with comments
on her artistry and choice of color.

        In actuality,
they are screaming at her with dying voices.
Their sobs are slowly strangulated.
        They are begging for water.

She surveys her painted nails approvingly.
She is oblivious to the flowers' needs.

            She wraps her thoughts in herself
                and kills all things
            trying to thrive in her wake.

Dream Drifting

She drifts through a dream
        as curtains of darkness
                surround her velvet thoughts.

A sliver of light parts the curtains
        and grows ever larger in width.

        A hairy two-legged animal
        beckons her to enter his den.

She races away with just one backward glance.
        The curtains are closed once again.

        Now she is flying through alien space:
        Nothingness, void, everywhere.
        A twinkling light in the distance
                swims closer.

        She hovers, dream drifting above
        a city of golden carved pyramid wings.
                A blindingly, beautiful sight.

        She hovers in thought then pivots
        and flies through yellow-green circles.
                Barriers break.
        The curtains of darkness melt.

        She exits her surreal circles and colours
        into reality's saw-edged squares
        and hazy monochrome themes.

                Time shifts
        and the dream dissolves.

Blue Days

She does the brown chores of blue days.

> Golden hours of imagination
> salvage the murky minutes.

Introspective questionnaires
> flood her fantasy forest.

> *Why is she constantly surrounded
> by brown chores?*

Continuing the annihilation of brown chores,
> she signs a declaration
embosses it on her cranial countryside.

> *What most she seems;
> that least she is.*

Blue days and brown chores are not affected
by this never-ending autumn season.

> Their colour remains —
> constant.

Actions

Sometimes, she feels
      she's genuine Hollywood material;
especially after one of her many dramatic scenes
      she performs for him.

    He thinks she's a bitch.

      He doesn't realize
    she's just another frustrated
      would be actress.

She must be pretty good
if he doesn't realize her true intentions.

      Roles and substitutions
      are all she's ever known.

Bible Story

When I was a youngster,
        I had a couple of bibles.
            One was dark blue.
The other was covered in tiny artificial pearls.

I never read them
        and I never needed them
                because I was just a kid.

I'm older now,
        and I don't have even one bible.

        I need one now.
        Any colour would do.
        Any colour at all.

I don't even have enough money
        to buy one tomorrow.

It's funny
how you never miss what you've lost
        until you really need it.

Maybe I'll be able to buy a bible next week —
        If I still need one, then.

Graven Images

I can't believe I'm still here,
        underground,
trapped in the damp soil of my grave.

I've always been pretty good at guessing time.
I think it's been over twenty-four hours now
and I'm still down here in the darkness.

        I can't get out
and nobody has come for me.
        I can't even hear
anybody whispering for me.

I wonder, when I died,
if there was some colossal screw-up
or if the death registrar was sleeping?

Anyhow,
    I know something's wrong.
    I never thought it would be like this.
    I always thought there was:
        Something.
        Somewhere.
        Somehow.

I don't know what's worse:
        The numbing nothingness.
        Or the deafening silence.

I guess worms don't dig this deep,
        And...
I guess I was wrong.

Entrances

I never know how to greet him anymore
        when he walks through the door.

If I rush to his arms
        and give him my heat
        he usually tears it apart.

            If I give him an inch
            he takes ten thousand miles.

            If I give him a mile
            he's off on a star flight.

If I glance at him coolly
        and call him a name
        he usually sits up like a dog;
        but sometimes he reacts
            completely opposite
            to my expectations.

I never know how to greet him anymore
        when he walks through the door

So, I've decided not to be home when he arrives.

        That way,
            he can try to figure
            the right way to greet me
            when I walk through the door.

The Absence of Sound Waves

Every face I see
    is a grey blanket of despair.
Depression from the mouths that speak
    from time to time
        dissolve eras betwixt.

    Ages pass like marble games
    played with steelies, cobs and purees.

    The cat's-eyes were all won
        by some unlucky finger
        or by a dummy disguised.

Was the game played with finger drawn circles
    or little earth dugouts?

    I try to visualize the field
        between wall to wall
            faces of grey despair.

All that's left are gravel roads.
    The streets and boulevards
    sickened of the grey faces
and boarded a rocket to a brighter world.

    If there had been radio contact
    I might have been able to follow them.

    My receiver resounds
    in perpetual silence.

A Song is a Song

Black bonded paper
        and transparent ribbons
        are typing a note in the air

It's almost like an invisible plane
        skywriting without any fuel.

It's funny how you can know things
without reading, seeing, or hearing.

It's strangely comparative
        to braille of the brain.
                Sensory receptors
                tuned or untuned
        still pick up sound waves of sorts.

It's all in the way you decipher the code

        A rhapsody to one
        is acid rock to another.

        And,
           a song
                is a song,
                      is a song.

Temporary Jailbird

Inside out now and upside down
           I gaze through my cell bars.
        Dragged from my home sweet home
           by two blue uniforms.
I found an unmade bed.

The yellow stripe made those two nice guys
made them seem like regular everyday assholes.
I thought maybe I was in the middle of a dream;
      a bizarre uninvited nightmare.
My feet were freezing without my warm fleece boots
I couldn't figure out why they took them from me.

Lying on a slab of cold concrete
I stared at my very own porcelain potty.

           Above me
another slab of concrete that didn't look too sturdy.

       I remember thinking,
if I receive a roommate, I'll shift to the upper bunk
because if that suspended weapon ever weakened
I would be nothing but crushed bone marrow
       in a matter of seconds.

Through numerous one-sided interrogations
my only words were, "I have nothing to say."

Eventually, my crusader, my saviour, my lawyer
      shuffled into the station house.
      Ten minutes later
I walked into the ice-chilled atmosphere
      in my fleece boots.

      Released at last.
My God, the chill felt different!

Windows, Cupboards and Bizarre Brown Chairs

We were cleaning the kitchen windows
when they suddenly changed into cupboards.

I found a small basket containing
a bunch of half-chewed jap-orange remains.
As I dumped them in the garbage
I noticed the brown living room chair
had become semi-human.
It was rocking back and forth
and trying to stand up.

We went to have a smoke in the living room
and I saw the chair turn its head toward me.
There was a little creature in a white shirt
cramped into the corner.

>*I yelled at you to look at the chair;*
>*that it was alive.*

You looked at me as if I was crazy;
       so, I touched it and it screamed.
I could still feel it's cold jelly-like essence
       as I ran to the back door.

I hugged you tight and tried to tell you I was sorry
       but I had lost my voice.

You said you always thought that chair was evil.
    You said we would have to get rid of it
              ... soon.

Silent Dream

I wrote my words on the wind
        and spoke through the lips of a star.

The sky was listening so intently for a scream,
        somehow, it missed my whisper.

Circular etchings of a long-lost song
        were sung through a ray of light
        and became a speck of dust,
        bio-degradable in essence
        yet infinite in dexterity.

I showered under
        the white purifying rain of belief
        and washed all my sins away.

        The gale winds calmed,
        the stars shone bright
            and the sky —

the sky was a silent dream.

Ninety-Six Eyes

Ninety-six eyed green monster of joy.

You stare at me through the open-faced
    spiral staircase banister.

Your arms are too numerous
    for me to count them correctly
    but still, you don't frighten me
      you fill me with warmth
      and a feeling of peace.

I hung you with happiness
    and trimmed you with trinkets.

What would Christmas be
    without your twinkling eyes
      and tinsel laden arms?

    Ninety-six eyes
radiating the spirit of Christmas.

Tarantula Trek

Mystic followers of the west wind sequel
        we travel. dissuaded shadows.
        in search of redeeming shades,

        Smiling faces ask no questions,
        peering out from inside their mirrors
            of red redemption.

        We've been searching foreign factories
        looking for the mechanical Christ
        who, in one swift motion,
        can absolve all our primary sins.

        We are the lonely singers
            making noise
        on our lost spider-webbed shores,
          seeking a holy baptismal.

Mystic followers
        of a mad musical menagerie
        we are hypnotized
        by the tarantula's dance
        and forever caught in
        her unforgiving web.

Replacements

Finger snapping brain waves
seem somehow out of tune these days
just like mara-bones and pickaninny gum;

Heavy acid rockers
        are lost on the waves of disco drum rolls
              and,
        some sneak has oiled
        each and every one of their fingers.

        They couldn't snap out of it
        even if they wanted to.

Hand clapping nerve endings
are obliterating all the phalange fallacies
        we've been led to believe.

Looking through my binoculars
I see a semi-submerged
hand in the ocean.

I can almost hear the dull thud
of its futile fingers
snapping and slapping;
thwapping and splashing.
wanting to crack and pop,
smack and hard tap.

The current sound effects don't cut it
replacements are required.

A City Sleeping

It was five forty-five A. M.
    My car rambled through
    the sleeping Vancouver streets.

    There was no traffic on Hastings.
    The cars had crashed
    in the garages of their dreams.

    The sometimes drivers were comatose.
    The street was deadly deserted.

    The cold grey buildings
    loomed grotesquely
    against the gradual skyline.

The signal lights seemed inappropriately awake
    in their semi-silent clicking state.

    Old run-down theatres,
        decrepit department stores,
        skid row hotels
        and random restaurants
            scampered from my sight
            as my vehicle vaulted
        through the silent streets
of a sleeping city.

    Vancouver fell asleep
        one nuclear night

    — unawake and unaware —

        Such a quiet death.

Iceberg Horses

Galloping over too high fences
       the horses are falling helplessly
       to their broken leg graves.

Before the gem encrusted gravel is heaped over them,
       buzzards chew the plastic bones
       protruding from their lame limbs.

       Swallows sing sorrowfully.
The stars blink back tears with every twinkle.

     Dawn,
   crawling in blindly,
focuses on the reflection of dewdrops
   from the dead equestrian eyes:

       Red roses of the tundra
          stirred into
       ice-cooled beverages.

       Icebergs collide in their wake
          of glowing darkness.

       Night whispers of mortality.

Artificial Eyes

Joe and Mary
are hoping for a change in the weather
        and the scenery.

He wants to trade in their old bicycles
        for a trip to Hawaii.
She wants to buy a new car
        with her shopping coupons.

        Instead,
they tear down their flopped angel cake house
        and build a tent
  with extra chocolate icing
they never would have used anyway.

Mary washes fading moonbeams
        in her portable sink
        and promises herself
a brand-new custom-made wardrobe
fashioned with peppermint-cream chocolates.

Joe wakes in the morning and makes hourly plans
        for the rest of their lives,
        writes them down carefully
        with invisible ink.

He drinks his coffee through a straw:
        Doesn't want too much too fast.

        Mary sees a sunset.
        Joe sees a sunrise.

    In the eye of their hurricane
all that's visible are storm clouds.

Alive for a Day

He spits to the sky,
        potent saliva,
                alive for a day.

Small in anger,
        he walks slowly
                through a year.

        He must jump
                arranging wrists and elbows
                on the platter of his dreams.

Everything comes his way.
Unholy water on his head.
        Trees reach out to push him
        through the dying cycle.

He can't see what ears can hear,
        starved in white hope
            alive for a day.

His hot skin is freezing the sky,
but everything still comes his way
        to where the sky shouts obscenities
                and kills plants and animals.

He loses his head.
He walks in concrete shoes to the ocean.
He never knew he was going fishing.

        The day ends.
        So does he.

Music Spheres

She lies on a cushion of air.
    The music swirls around her
        like a Jacuzzi.

    Jets of mystical steam
    escort her to the stars.
        She floats
on a Milky Way magic carpet ride.

    The universe is midnight blue
    with black overtones.
    The stars are like a traffic jam
        in a black-out:
Cars turning and veering.
        Flickering signals.
Disappearing headlights.

    She threads her way through them
        like a mobile needle.

Her electric propelled carpet
moves supersonically.

    Everything is unclear,
        unfocused,
    a split-second blur.

        She passes everything
        and sees nothing.

    She doesn't mind.
    The music is all that matters.

Many Dreams Ago

Soup always gives him a fever
and ice-cream makes him cough.

      Whiskey gives him a hang-over
      and cigarettes calm his nerves.

He is a perfect example
of a screwed-up metabolism.

      He sleeps quite a lot
      so he doesn't have to talk.

He drinks quite a lot
as he can't face the truth.

      He is not himself.
He is only a crepe paper picture
    of what he used to be
      many dreams ago.

Suspension Bridge

With a theory of pyramids in his eyes,
he measures the golds and blues.

Teething on orange and green crackers,
he's a Hallowe'en hand-out surprise.

Egyptian tapestries cover his shoulders.

The molecular structure of pyramid dust,
blowing and flowing through
time-lapse suspension,
erects an unstable bridge.

The bridge collapses,
falling over the future
down dusty trails
hiding the past.

Theoretically,
he's proven his blue eyes
to be golden triangles of truth
digesting his broken dreams.

      His teeth
  have tasted the dust.

Bathroom Blues

He's a book of pages.

Lids lowered,
       sleep slowly receding,
       he saunters into the bathroom.

Repetitiously he rubs his weary eyes.
      He focuses fumblingly
      at his haggard reflection.

            A stranger,
           resembling himself,
           stares blankly
           from inside the mirror.

When did the sparse grey hairs
      begin to lengthen their gap?

When did the crinkled crows' feet
      begin to perch so comfortably
      at the corners of the eyes?

           When did the youthful laughing eyes
           begin to lose their sparkle?

           When did the final chapter begin?

Sewn

His eyes are open
wide as a sunrise.

His lips are parted and glistening
like sensuous crystal dewdrops.

He runs his flaming fingers
through her waterfall hair.

Their mouths negotiate the birth
of a new and rapturous language.

      Their bodies
are one slow moving act of love.

There is no moment of doubt;
no questions of mind or flesh.

Invisible hands have sewn
the garment of their hearts together
in a golden masterpiece of wings.

Flying through rainbows and love songs,
they elude the shuffle of sundown.

The Winds of Change

Write the last page first
and centre the beginning.
      Let your days flow unevenly
      in constant wavering confusion.
Edge all your pages with black hope
and plot your way out of the present.

When you reach the past,
survey the architecture with a blind eye
so the seen will never threaten
      the things you want to see.

Begin your journey to oblivion
in torn and tattered shoes.
Walk with a limp
and search your soul
for a crutch.

When your search is ended
your life will begin its termination;
      and, as the end is in sight,
      with ferocious fervor,
      bolt back to the starting line.

When you are on your mark
      and set to go,
patiently await the silence crumbling
to the crack of the starting pistol...

      and then,
      the race is on.

Blotters

We are the lustful giants
when it comes to sex.

      We are the paranoid pygmies
      when it comes to understanding.

I dance to a different set of principles.
Your drum beats with a different brand of morals.

It's a good thing
you're a statue of perpetual passion,

or I'd be a portrait
      of a disappearing Diana.

We are the blended ink stains
      of some bizarre Rorschach test:

      A look-alike blotter
        of opposites.

Showers and Dust

I jumped out of the shower
and wrapped my multi-coloured towel
over my socially un-exposable parts.

I towelled outside
to take the dog I never had
for a walk.

He was telephone high-wire walking,
    but his twenty-five-foot leash
    was dragging on the ground.

We walked for miles:
    He above.
    I below.

How noble and nimble the performing pooch was.
    He never faltered a paw.

I stumbled on a few pugnacious pebbles
    and disintegrated to dust:
the cleanest, freshly showered dust on the beach.

Hammers and anvils and stirrups
can hear the canine's desperate cry;

but I can't rescue him ....
    I can't get my dust together.

These Wolves

The wolves we fed
        wait outside
        chained to their howls
                and stalked by our moon.

I can hear their claws
        scratching on the sidewalk;
        and their breath circling our dreams
            like a noose —
                a noose tightening.

        I am the hangman.
        You're the executioner;

        And they are our jailers ...
            these wolves.

AUTHOR PROFILE

Candice James is a professional poet, musician, singer, songwriter, and visual artist. She was appointed Poet Laureate Emerita of New Westminster BC by order if City Council in November 2016 after serving 2 back-to-back three-year terms as Poet Laureate. She is founder of Royal City Literary Arts Society, and Fred Cogswell Award for Excellence in Poetry and past president of the Federation of BC Writers. She's a full member of the League of Canadian Poets and the author of 31 books of poetry through 6 Publishing Houses.

She has been published internationally in magazines, periodicals, anthologies, and reviews. Her awards include Pandora's Collective Citizen of the Year; and Chamber of Commerce Bernie Legge Platinum Awards Artist of the Year.

www.ingramcontent.com/pod-product-compliance
Lightning Source LLC
Chambersburg PA
CBHW071248070526
44583CB00017B/2383